CABELANDS SERVICE AREA
ENO RIVER STATE PARK
AUTHORIZED VEHICLES ONLY

BRIDGE
RULES
DO NOT RUN.
SIT. JUMP.
OR PLAY
ON BRIDGE

Check out my other books available.

CREATIVE CAKES

BEAUTIFUL CAKES

MISC RAMBLING

FLOWER PICTURES

BEAUTIFUL FLOWERS

MISC RAMBLING

RICHMOND VA

CITY OF RICHMOND

MISC RAMBLING

BEAUFORT NC

FORT MACON STATE PARK

MISC RAMBLING

NATCHEZ TRACE

CLASSIC CARS

MISC RAMBLING

NASHVILLE TN

ARCHITECTURE DOWNTOWN

MISC RAMBLING

NASHVILLE TN

LAND BETWEEN THE LAKES

MISC RAMBLING

ANDERSONVILLE NATIONAL HISTORIC SITE

JIMMY CARTER NATIONAL HISTORIC SITE & MORE!

MISC RAMBLING

NC STATE FAIR

2012

MISC RAMBLING

The end.